Exiled Moon

*Olga
shining light
de nuestra Comunidad!
Amor y Paz
Naomi Quiñonez*

By Naomi Helena Quiñonez

12/8/2018

Copyright © 2017 by Naomi Helena Quiñonez.
Photographer: Michelle Gutiérrez Leyva
Artist: Pola Lopez

Library of Congress Control Number:		2017915388
ISBN:	Hardcover	978-1-5434-5737-7
	Softcover	978-1-5434-5738-4
	eBook	978-1-5434-5739-1

All rights reserved. No part of this book may be reproduced or transmitted in any form or by any means, electronic or mechanical, including photocopying, recording, or by any information storage and retrieval system, without permission in writing from the copyright owner.

Any people depicted in stock imagery provided by Thinkstock are models, and such images are being used for illustrative purposes only.
Certain stock imagery © Thinkstock.

Print information available on the last page.

Rev. date: 12/01/2017

To order additional copies of this book, contact:
Xlibris
1-888-795-4274
www.Xlibris.com
Orders@Xlibris.com
765329

Exiled Moon
Table Of Contents iii

Sometimes The Moon v

NEW MOON — 1

Circles Of Women 2
Lemon Drop Luna 6
Pumpling Heart 8
Long Lit Ladies 10
Lip Service 12

TIDAL WAVES — 15

Mama Mar 16
To The Last Drop 18
The Water Has Spoken 21
Redemption Exemption 22
In Cuba 24
Elemental 25
Dementias Of Culture 28
My Ear Ring 30

BLOOD MOON — 33

Voices Of The Old South 34
Bumping Into Walls 37
Breath Of Bone 39
The Poet's Grip 42
Connected 45

ECLIPSE 47

When You Look At Me: A Brown Woman's Lament 48
A Thin Line 51
The Babe The Bitch And The Bruja 53
Walls At Midnight 55
A Day In Mid Maya 57
A Rock Is Thrown 59
The Walk 62

WOLF MOTHER MOON 71

All Day 72
Torn 74
A Curse A Blessing 76
The Home 79
Tlazolteutl 82

PENUMBRA 85

Cosmic Pump 86
The Old Cantos 88
Coyote Calls 90
Lady Of Lost Causes 92
Just This Once 94
Ceremony Coyolxauqui 95
Ceremonia Coyolxauqui 97

Sometimes The Moon

Sometimes the moon
tells us stories
but we don't hear them

Sometimes the moon
divulges her secrets
to the night
but we don't listen

Sometimes the moon
waits in shadow
to pour her tales
into our dreams,
but we ignore them

We have forgotten
the language
of stars
and the moon's
ancient tales
about death and dying
and remembrance

The old stories
about how wounds
are made and healed
and how the essence
of our unruly lives
does not vanish
at daybreak

Forgetfulness exiles
the divine feminine
from the cool, creative
indigo twilight
of consciousness

To a sun struck
broken world
a mania of manipulated
masculinities
and endless destructions
in the stark light of day.

NEW MOON

Circles Of Women

Circles of women surround me.
they brush sorrows
off my shoulders
like dust
and sprinkle moon water
on my face
so that I may wake to dreams
of my own designs.

Our circle is a round mouth
laced in red lipstick
and laughter.
half moon smiles spill out
candle light, sage smoke
copal.

We speak heart-beat
to each others
unique palpitations
small vibrations
gather as one.

We remember
the bruised
broken faces
that reside in our fears.

We sort out futility
from power
and piece together new truths
from the discarded fabric
of old pain.

We see the greatest lies
intermingled
with the highest truths

We hold flesh
to moonlight
and hear
the muffled sounds
of wounds healing.

We utter the sacred songs
written into the hands
of the four directions.

A circle of small moons spinning
into a smoking vortex
we invoke la diosa
a hallow throat opens
and swallows us.

We are the entrails of mother earth
fires lap at our heels
winds howl like restless coyotas
rivers of sweat roll down our stomachs
our feet root
in a mulch of earth and bones.

Dis-ease drains out of
wounded hearts and weary bodies
into the loving earth.
we heal, we heal, we heal.
we are planted in a mixture
of earth and bone and memory.

We tell our stories
sing our songs
bless and cleanse
and invoke.

spirit of the east
place of new beginnings
your winds brush our faces!
carry our prayers
to the universe
bring us wisdom
on your wings.

spirit of the south
we invoke your vitality!
ignite our red-flame passion
fuel our desire
for justice and love.

spirit of the west
slack our thirst
for knowledge!
refresh our spirits
with cleansing waters.

spirit of the north
nuestra madre tierra
we honor you,
press our foreheads earth
take in your energy
and ground in compassion.

Circles of women surround me
they brush sorrows
off my shoulders
like dust
and sprinkle moon water
on my face
so that i may wake to dreams
of my own designs.

Lemon Drop Luna

Luna you
lemon drop
your shimmer sheet
cape of gold
across a tossing
reckless sea

Your pockmarked belly
lowers lightly
and taps
a blinking
urban island

Buttery light
yellow melon rhythms
play in burnt dust
of edgy cities

Gold corn woman
your cosmic cha cha
is the dance I dance
and the beat I follow

Moon groupie me
my tribal moments
trace your steps

the long walks
the old songs
under your saffron veil

I am tied to you
by blood and journey
the virgin's bleeding
he maidenhead broken
the sticky scarlet
of a newborn's head
the path from blood to light.

Round and round
dark to new
half to full
and round again

Glowing diosa
mandala mama
curried spiral
I love to move to

Spill your light
glowing diosa!
pull my body
like an ancient wave

Drop your luminescent
power
on my waiting
wanting
waxing
soul

Pumpling Heart

Murmur of love
upbeat and open
palpable breath-beat
of ocean waves.

Delicious fruit
pumpling heart
blue\red
tempo of
cosmic breath.

My place with you
on this unraveling planet
is on the back of
Coyolxauqui
celestial sprinter
into time.

Let's ride her spinning
integrations
her full moon cycles
her spatial chaos
her galactic soul.

Let's stir her into
steaming coffee
sip her magic
feel her force.

Let's taste her spirit
ingest her soul
as she makes her way
to our chambers
of flesh and light.

Long Lit Ladies

For Yolanda

This is the moment
long lit ladies
live for
lilting palma trees
sway in the afternoon.

Cabello envuelto
en sombra
y canción
senos, maracas
cocos dulces
cuerpos, curvas
peligrosos

Camino entre
hierbas altas
fresco, verde
dulce luz
long lit ladies
love to taste.

We share
Diosa
like water
flowing
from the same cup.

Bright bellies
burn like lamps
hearts ignite
a dance is born.

Lip Service

the pale-lipped sand
lays sideways
on the shore's grainy
bottom
beneath
a soft white beam
of moon's light

a sudden utterance
of divine
pays lip service
to the stars
and mundane bits
of light
transform into
a glamour of
glitterous terrain

at that moment
something coughs,
loose grains
take flight
into the windy night

some travel to distant places
and wind up as dust
on mountaintops

some take refuge in
cramped places
until they become
pearls

TIDAL WAVES

Mama Mar

i don't blame you
for your thrust and tumble
the rumble
inside your skin
i do not blame
your sweep and swallow
your shallow to deep
your pull and push
against the islands
of despair

i do not blame
your megaton waves
your steel-blade foam
your wet red sands

i can only contemplate
great energies
released
and give the dead
their due

watch the steady stream
of dreams passing
into an aftermath
where all things
become one

plastic and elastic
shards of mosque
tires and silver forks
soggy shoes
lap tops and table tops
doors and ruined books

around the limp bodies
of children
a million cell phones swirl
the batteries
dead too

all swollen
into one mixture
of our precious lives
and junk

i do not blame you
for stiff blue fingers
that stab the air
or the eyes that float
in the angry surf

only for the awe
that wakes me
like the pain
that breaks me
to the truth of you

To The Last Drop

We have dropped
black, oily
poisons
into a tunnel
of churning water

We have dropped
blood
like dirty bombs
into the womb
of mother earth

We drop
our drawers
to bend over
for the gang rape
of capital

Production lines
and pensions
fall into archived memory
classified
for maximum
dropage

The constitution
drops
like an old tattered
love letter
from a numb
feeble hand

We are dropping
dropping, dropping
into an abyss
of our own making

With our own hands
we pull the lever
to flush ourselves down
the swirling toilet bowl

The passage of shit,
is slow an laborious
the passage of light
limitless

Why are we dropping
dropping
dropping,
why are we dropping
like flies?

Earth falling
fires burning
wind exploding
water dripping
dropping onto
rotted floorboards,
flooded warlords

at the door?

Someday soon
our bodies will drop
heavy, wet
bathing suits
to the floor

Falling, falling
we drop
some more

Soon there will
be nothing
to hold
us up

The Water Has Spoken

The water has spoken
lashing tongue
of destruction
there is no obstruction
to her power.

Broken bodies
between her teeth
futures lie
beneath the ravaged
sand.

Death
provides no relief
from what ails
the human mind.

Flesh is separated
by color and creed
but the collective brain
boils from the need
to understand
the ocean's
harsh words.

In the end
our inept and futile
interpretations
only negate
lives lived
on the borrowed
breath of illusion.

Redemption Exemption

Today the fires burn
orange tongues lap
the crisp skin
of singed metro valleys

History's pretty dressings
come undone
to reveal
rot worn wounds
burrowed in the tough skin
of arrogance

There have been
too many boots
and bayonets
in our collective faces

A glut of blood
clotting battlefields
and sidewalks

Too much iron
and too much fire
and too much
force of will

Inflamed winds
engulf the manicured lawns
of our fragile ecologies

And so the fires blaze
hot, insistent mirrors
reflect Persia's
burned faces
alive and smoldering
in suburban sprawl

The heat hitting hard
and the soul searching
absently
for the cool wet casings
of redemption

In Cuba

In cuba
people line
the furtive
boulevard
of the malecon
barricade
of barnacles
riveted
to the sea
imagining
something
other
than wet
other
than blue
measuring
distant
geographies
with outstretched
eyes
straining
for the histories
that make them
anxious
for the fluidity
of passing
clouds

Elemental

Elemental
the horse's hooves
the inconvenient
racetrack

Big brown
is down

A limp bank
whimpers
so much potential
so little hope

Bended
diasporas
legislated
dictatorships
fuel the falling future

Morals migrate
into drifting spaces
moguls mark
their territory

A world of weird
markings
viscosity of death
everywhere

How well can we tell
the yes from the no
the today from tomorrow?

Its on t.v.
proof
testing positive
for fatal dis-ease

A waste of water
rushes
incubating disasters
dislodge
winds swoop
100,000 disappear

This is the time we live in
a shiny vortex of fear
beneath each shaky home

Climb a skyscraper

A corporate coffin
coughs blood
bleeds oil

Sun burnt suits
and pale skulls
conspire
You can bet on it!

In
vestments
high priests
raise the
stakes

Altars of
capital gains
shatter teeth
starve lungs

False profits
ride the downward
spiral

Tomorrow
a collection
of frozen body parts
dislocated eyes
hair splintered with hate

The rush hour news
broadcasts
a traffic jam
of lives

Stay tuned for doom

Dementias Of Culture

Dementias of culture
whirl through
old hallways
the smell of deaf
and dumb on the
walls.

Forgotten tribes
tribulate inside
ironclad foreheads
steelhead trout.

Brother
leave the brooks brother
to the plaster of paris
and dump the trump cards.

Sister
wash your hair
in the river
and practice
your bold
new songs.

Too soon the dementias
of culture will forget
to introduce us.

Too soon a hungry vulture
will have us disappeared
from the spot
that runs.

My Ear Ring

time is disappearing
poles are shifting
glaciers are melting
oceans are heating
volcanoes exploding
mountains sliding
air evaporating
land is losing
light is dimming
men manipulating
media minds
meandering

lawyers are looting
our children are shooting
developers polluting
the doctors are drugging
the papers are plugging
politicians lying
the president spying
the government is dying
winds are crying
land will not be drying

the schools are closing
principals posing
students are supposing
the end is near

dealers are winning
the elite class whining
workers not working
poor are pouring
into pits of warring

the water is wasting
oil men taking
priests are raping
boys shaking
bodies caking
hearts are breaking

the trees are toppling
birds are dropping
fish are frying
torturers are tying
soldiers are burning
and not returning
souls are hurting
mothers grieving
churches deceiving

war lords are stealing
women need healing
hatred is killing
millionaires milling
billionaires billing
the gulf is boiling
migrants are toiling
cheap labor
exploiting

the white house
is sinking
the P.R. is stinking
senators winking
cocktail glasses tinkling

humanity is reeling
faces are peeling
the drug dealers
dealing
the dead have no feeling

clocks are ticking
dogs are licking
congress is tricking
the house dividing
the people fighting
thieves are picking
democracy sickening

the past is haunting
the present mocking
the future is daunting

My stocking is running
my resolve should be stronger
I could live longer

My ear is ringing
lovers are loving
jokers are punning
the children are grinning
love light is pinning
a new beginning
for the saved & the sinning
the self and the other
the father and mother
the guide and the guardian
the children's sweet pardon

the singer's soft song
rose light of dawn
the me and the you
a polished red shoe
the false and the true
a witches' sweet brew.
The changes are due.

BLOOD MOON

Voices Of The Old South

Voices of the old south
bellow in the new wind
the ghosts of slave owners
commandeer media
monitor the masses
for hate.

The ku klux klan
casts off their sheets
and storms the
streets of Washington.

A body of white
and bellicose
in sweat pants
and tennis shoes
parades its scorn,
spits in the face
of reason
and marches to the
legacy of the hate
that seeded
this nation's
power.

Centuries
of Jim crow
native genocides
continuous
dispossession of
Mexicans
and anti immigrant
sediment.

Decades
of indentured
servitudes
have carved
harsh hearts,
hardened the thin
interiors of souls
craving the violent
controls of the past.

What are you
but a lynch mob
in patriot's clothing
set out to hang
the future by its neck
longing to leer
with sweaty eyes
at a social body
swinging from
a noose?

March on
dwindling cadavers
your threats
to exterminate
are pointless stagings
of your fear
Of new winds blowing
louder and stronger
with the voices
of ALL people
whose blood
has nourished
this land.

Bumping Into Walls

We followed
that hallowed wall
the black one
that stole our image
as we traced
the braille
of a million
names

That loud wall
gave us passage
to a secret wound
into which we bled

There below
the feet of Abe
the air tasted of
Gettysburg
and smelled
of fall leaves
burning
under a winter
of empty coats

A rattling rush
of battered hearts
drummed unwanted truths
into our ears

We heard a sad verse
of earthen bodies
of mud drying
to hard clay
and voices that said
there are brothers and sisters
who speak
to shadows
and let sprits
inhabit their tongues

We followed
the stuttering syllables
and saw death repeated
on an eternal battlefield
from which the ghosts
of men and women return

We heard battered words
and bruised prayers
for a time
that will turn
combat zones
into meadows
and war cries
into poetry

Breath Of Bone

a breath of bone
hangs in the air

onslaught
of thievery
atrocities
chained to
limp dicks
that line
the walls
of congress

defiled democracies
and supply side
theocracies
control the show

god is a puppet
pulled by thin strings
who sings
the colonial slogans
of power, of will
and the will to power
of puppets posing as
god.

world trap
global travesty
suck the
possibility of evolution
from the sagging bones
of tomorrow

captains of dust
clutch clouds
by the throat
rounds of random
aggression
fire into temples
sacred places
ransacked

the fist
like the mind
always clenched.

(bombs are not dirty
men are)

streets
of vibrant possibility
struggle towards light
but are darkened
by the stamp of boots
on ancient faces.

I send the love
that so many die for
I search for opened eyes
in the faces
of poppies that grow
on pale hills

I pan for some small hope
in the clogged streams
of invasion
and pray for the
hard rain of reason

The Poet's Grip

Corrugated
silence
shadows
the pierced skin
of innocents

Time drolls
darkly in some
smelly cell
the kind that keeps
the keeper's context
on death row

One for all
and for destruction!
the banter goes
deep

Centuries of DNA
pour into
sterile fields
of war

Who are we to stand up
to confiscated futures
or resist
insistent sabers

stuck halfway
to the heart?

Who am I to know
the secret of the
stars and hands
constellations
spread across
a human palm,
the anatomy
of tomorrow?

Hard walls
edge between
fabricated fiestas
of failure
and the long wails
that line yet
another trail of tears

Soldiers empty
tired veins into
barrels of black
and blister

Camouflage
of fear
humanity
put on hold

Someday soon
it will find us
and demand
what has been taken

I wet the hollow center
of my poets grip
with the spit
of terrorized histories

And write the lost
verses of evolution
on the rough pages
of decay

Connected

We are all connected
to the belly of the earth
each soul kicking-out
flames fed by the heat
of magma, lava and crust.
Millions of umbilical cords
tied to a common center.

We are a bouquet of flowers
balloons and bellies
that cannot escape
each others breath
cannot escape
each other's divine
imperfect lives
or profane
and comic deaths.

This is how I know the pain
of flesh sliced to pieces
by instigated metal
cutting through air
to make its mark
on children huddled
in futile corners
of scattered rubble.

This is how I feel
the twisted gut-wrenched war cry
in the torn stomachs of women
who watch loved ones
explode into heaps of useless ash
yesterday's frightened eyes
melted into pockets of charred skin.

This is how I see
a civilization disappear
under a blood-stained blanket
another piece of humanity
ripped out of the womb
of mother earth,
another dream of peace
raped at gunpoint.

My belly is a heavy weight
I carry into the uncertainty
of each hesitant day,
my heart a bruised eruption
of haphazard futures.

The center tugs hard
yanks the collective heart
clears the common eye
pulls the blood
from our tangled veins.

and if you say
that you don't feel this
you are lying.

ECLIPSE

When You Look At Me: A Brown Woman's Lament

When you look at me
you see motel maids
changing sheets
in the pink & grey rooms
your parents stay in.

you see dark brown women
on their knees scrubbing floors
in Baja restaurants
or standing with a blue-eyed child
on each hip.

It doesn't matter if I wear
tweed suits and pace the floor
on Givenchy heels
in front of busy chalk boards

You see Lupita the nanny
in your t.v. mind.
she wears mismatched clothes
and slides heavily on leather huaraches
towards her unwashed children.

To you I am an aberration
that confuses your senses
and blurs your vision.
It is difficult for you to
recognize me as "Dr."
You want me to remain nameless
silent, invisible.

But I stand before you
speaking your language
and teaching you things
you are not sure of.

Now you must either change
your misguided notions of who I am
or kill the me
that cannot live in your world.

II

When you look at me
you see educated nipples
intelligent legs, a brilliant ass.

You chica, mija, chula me
until you get beyond the fact
that i have a phd.

In department meetings
I call for broad visions
and student needs.
You envision a broad
who can meet your needs.

You are unfamiliar
with a woman
who can see through
your veneer.
My loud clear voice
threatens your ears.

To you I am expendable
like the woman who keeps
taking you back
like the mother who is
always there to feed you.

Like that part of yourself
that you thought you destroyed
when you decided to become
a thin worn metallic chair
a conflict without a resolution.

A Thin Line

for the women of Juarez

It is a wide desert
and a thin line
thin as ropes
that bind the wrists
of undernourished women

It is a vast plain
of unmitigated history
and a slim knife
that cuts off the breasts
of would-be mothers

It is a mother lode
of corporate profit
and a ribbon of
bleeding throats

It is a mass grave
of terror and rape
and a small slice
of our uncertain futures

It is large enough
to hide the bones
of suffocated women
but not quiet enough
to stifle
their cries

Kill us when you can
torture us when you can
bury us if you can

But the spirits of women
who die in battle
will return
as fierce
hummingbirds

winged warriors
of history
hovering memory
of your
forgotten humanity

A border is only
an imaginary line
all hearts
are the center
of the universe

The Babe The Bitch And The Bruja

Babe: see
boobs, breasts, bombshell, bimbo
breathless, butt, beaten, bathing beauty
belly, burdened, boxed, bent, busty
bare, beautiful, backward, bait, balled
bawdy, bedspread, bedroom, bed
beguiled, betrayed, blank, brief
bruised

Bitch: see
bite, bombastic bold, belligerent
brutal, bent, boisterous, ballsy
bisexual, bossy, banal, brat. Braggart
backbone, ballistic, bulldoze
brave, bad, badger, battle, bashed,
beer, besieged, blade, blatant, bellicose
boast, brawl, brazen, bristle, buttress
bruised

Bruja: see
breath, brainy, burnt, brilliant
brimstone, bone, buzz, baleful
brave, boiled, broomstick, blood
bells, breached, bite, beware,
bewitched, blasted, brew, blink
blow, bumped, burden
bound, blessed, broken, belief
bruised

Walls At Midnight

I want to rub myself
against an unfolding line
the one I follow
to those dark places

I want to place that
sweet meridian
in my mouth
and suck until
it explodes inside me

When I lean back
with eyes closed
I want to see the many roads
where travelers cross
and where centuries unravel

To feel the pulse of river
in my temples
and the taste of spice
on my tongue

I want to listen to
the common prayer
in the utterance
of all prayers
and to lick

the essence
of distant flowers
from the skin
wire fences.

Sad the line
it turns to rope
it is a harsh cord
yanked across a geography
of mute men and
the animated corpses
of women.

Whose border is this
anyway?
which side am I on?
why can't I just make
love to you
blur the lines
between heaven and hell
cure you of your bottom lines
round you off like a spiral
and make you mine?

A Day In Mid Maya

Snooty Maya
you drop
your words
like
water
on the desert
of my soul

you know the dance
of light and ego
its eternal
crystallized
trance

you know
earth smell
you touch
moon skin
you breathe
sun smoke

I like your style
cholo priest
lamb in wolf's
clothing

I like the mad
and I like the
the nomad

the moment
and the thing
beyond that

I like the play
of your
inland shadows
and the poem
that dangles
from
your earthy lips

A Rock Is Thrown

Once there were excuses
for boiling a women
in a pot
locking her up
to rot.

Accused witches
the fatally unclean
under moral strictures
that intervened
in the lives of women
who had to worry
about god, the husband
the secret juries.

peter peter pumpkin eater
had a wife and could not keep her
so he put her in a shell
and there he kept her very well.

Throw a witch
in deep water
if she drowns
she's the devil's daughter

Place her body
on a burning stake
if she burns
there's no mistake.

peter peter pumpkin eater
had a wife and could not keep her
so he put her in a cell
and there he kept her very well.

Today there is no need
for proof of evil
her existence alone
renders her feeble

Renders her useless
and /or expendable
to the needs of men
she is dependable

peter peter pumpkin eater
had a wife and could not keep her
so he put her
in a hell
and there he kept her very well.

Free of pretense
outside the law
the degenerate patriarch
slams its paw

To suffocate her ringing voice
to control her body
to limit choice

And if that does not
achieve the goal
of women's place
on the totem pole

Then bind her, beat her
slash her face
murder the source
of the human race

For no good reason
other than.
they have the power
and they can.

peter peter pumpkin eater
had a wife and could not keep her
so he put her in a shell
and there he has kept her very well.

The Walk

That morning
like every morning
Maria woke early
dressing quickly
to the dark metallic
rooster crow

A frayed sweater
slipped on hastily
nervous movements
jolting
a small frame
fragile
as packaged eggs

Maria uncovered
a rusty cage
from where
Pepito chirped
she sweet talked
the sunny canary
and she poured him water

Her time to smile
was short.

Desperate to arrive
there on time
she grabbed
a cold tortilla
anxiously kissed her
mother goodbye
and walked quickly
into the dark

By the time
the sun rose
between planks
of course smog
and smoke stained clouds
Maria reached
the edge
of her decayed
town.

It was a two-hour walk
a ten hour day
and two hours to return
from there
to the thin green shanty
her family occupied

She was like
hope hanging from
the family throat
a swinging
pendulum
of uncertainty
a small dark
pendant
of chance

15 cents an hour
staved off hunger
but the dark circles
tattooed under her eyes
told a story
too desperate
for a seventeen
year old girl

The long walk
in the desert
of her birth
felt heavy
that morning
the earth a
soft sponge
swallowed her legs
as she sank
into the porous sand.

When Maria finally
arrived there
perspiration drenched
limp black hair
a wrinkled blouse.

No!
she silently
screamed to herself
as her breath
quickly disappeared.

The massive
metal gates

slammed shut
before he
paralyzed eyes.

In the vertigo
of the moment
Maria heard
the deafening drone
of the malquiladora

Desperate to enter
she thought of
throwing herself
against the malquiladora's
clenched maw
but her legs sank
deeper
as if she were
disappearing
into the sand

On another day
Maria would have
rushed passed
the chrome barred
entrance
searching for her
friend Alma
among the hundreds
of dark haired women
confined as
potted plants

On another day
she would have

taken her place
at one of dozens
of long tables
laid out like dominos
across a cold
fluorescent floor

On another day
she would have grabbed
her grey smock
rubbed her mother's
special ointment
into her swollen hands
and lifted the heavy
metal staple gun

On another day
Maria would have spent
the next ten hours
in the airless
windowless box
of the general electric
company

On another day
after a robotic
announcement
ended her shift
and the voices of men
shouting orders
retreated to the back
of her mind
Maria would have joined
her friends
for the long walk home

But not today
Maria would
pay the price
for those 3 minutes
$1.50
a week's worth
of tortillas
or a gallon of water
a dozen eggs
or a bag of chiles
gone

Worse, another
incident
could replace her

they were all
replaceable
expendable
as machine parts.
Anxiety
insured a place
inside the
machine.

The desert's
eerie quiet
contained her
famished daze
as she left there
to start a dark
numb journey
back to her shanty

Pepito flew into her mind
his yellow feathers ruffling
his morning song
whistling in her head.

Maria is not sure
when she heard them
it started out as
the muffled sound
of a truck engine
carrying the distant
laughter of men

But soon,
too soon
the truck
the laughter
and the men
were on her

Maria startled
into consciousness
began to run
but she was
too far away
too far from
the malquiladora,
too far from
the shanty
too far from
her next breath.

Out of nowhere
a roped reached
to lasso her

she felt the drag
of sharp hot rocks
scrape against
her body
she saw the blood
she smelled the
fumes of oily exhaust
and she heard the
harsh insane shouts
of madmen.

Roars of hurled
brutality
and the ripping
of her clothes
by course hard hands
were the last sounds
she heard
but Maria
was never heard from
again.

The next morning
after a night of anguish
and a dawn of cruel grief
Maria's mother limply lifted
the cover of
the birdcage
and found Pepito's
yellowed lifeless body
on the seed strewn
cage floor.

WOLF MOTHER MOON

All Day

All day
the unresolved
issues
festered.
Past was shackled
to the present
by the hairs
of childhood
pulled out at the roots.
Luckless memory
of defiance
lingered,
a half century of skin
on bedroom doors.

The last time she saw
those restless eyes
and gnawing mouth
she was seven years old.

Words too harsh to swallow
were slammed dunked
into her ears
shrieks and screams
scattered
the suffocated air.

I walk behind
the drooping child
her small fists clenched
against the moment's turbulence.

I watch her enter
the schoolroom door
anxious
for the heavy heat
of knowledge.

Torn

I have torn your heart in half
with who I am
and I can never repay you

Sliding from between your
heaving thrusts
I reached to kiss the face of fear

Your reckless nature
made you quick with me
a dark explosion of you
is stamped in my eyes

Yesterday you told me
that you would have liked
to have stormed
the iron gates
of the patriarch

Instead
you felt trapped
inside its fortress walls
abandoned and desperate
to think
you could not flee

I was born in the belly
of your desperation
and longed to escape

I understand
I have known that fortress
and decided never to return.
Ours walls are ours alone

Time allows me
to put you in your
rightful place

There as a mother
who has loved
with teeth sharp
and eyes peeled
and whose darkness
helped me find
my own light

Even if our paths
are different
sometimes brutal
sometimes splendid
and always uneven

Does not mean we cannot speak
through the blood
that feeds our hearts

A Curse A Blessing

I cursed you
yesterday
tossed the past
at you
and watched
you fumble
into the voice
that has
been lying to you
for ages.

A tug of nerves
a case of wars
your madness
on my last
straw

Your frail bones
bristling
in an anger
never surrendered
karma coiled
around our hearts
tight

The heavy arms
of yesterday
push and pull
me in and out
of your orbit

Once you were
a mallet of bone
a box like
fortress of flesh

I could never climb
your parapet of
squandered fists
and heavy words

Time has diminished
the weight of your desires
and left you a thin shadow
a ghost inhabiting
a house of regret.

I'll never understand
never get it
never see you for
what you could have been
or what I needed.

But these eyes
that have watched you
tend the scars
that fester
tempestuously
on your heart

Today I light sage
and bring it to you
the fragrance opens
like your eyes

Me das un sumario?
you ask your restless
wandering daughter
who has traveled
time and distance
to collect these blessings

I wind the curling smoke
around your body
invoke the four directions
bless your feet
your hands your heart

You breathe
I breathe
past and present
disappear

We are just two women
struggling in the
here and now
seeking peace

Moving
beyond blood
beyond mother and daughter
fusing gently
to the sacred feminine
and the faint familiarity
of our souls.

The Home

in the home
on a chair
a woman
collapses
into a
home made
coma.

pesky memory
erased
and relieved
of its troublesome
duties place and time
black out

the woman
sits sullen
in between
lulls
picks
at her pants
and dribbles

her children
don't recognize her
anymore
her grandchildren

don't recognize her
anymore
her friends
don't recognize her
anymore

the home they
put her in
doesn't recognize her
anymore

the high class home
where nuns
keep time like little clocks
in black and white cloaks

tic toc
tic toc
the old
are dying
in the hallways
the doctors
far away

drug induced
stupors require
nothing but the best
for your elderly

don't know
what to do
with them?
trust us
to the tune
of $10,000

a month

the chairs
have wheels
but they don't
go anywhere

tic toc
tic toc
the old
are dying
in the hallways
the doctors far away

the chairs
have wheels
but they don't go
anywhere
nothing and no one
goes anywhere
in the home
of no return.

Tlazolteutl

The hurt is over
family secrets
spill on the table

*jewels strewn
among the wreckage
of memory*

Time is tethered
to a line of scar
between a child's
clutchings
and an ancient woman
dying back
into her pillow
of redemption

*listen to the miracle
inside a crumbling street
and the ghosts of
yesterday's children*

Have you ever
heard the rain
ever really heard it?

*a split of syllables
liquid lingo
of lost voices*

Have you ever
smelled the rain
heavy mist of mineral
and loam?

*a sheet of wet earth
an uncertain future
an unsteady present*

Have you ever
touched the rain
felt it transform
skin to silt?

*soft gems of light
scattered among
shards of remembrance*

Tlazolteutl - filth eater
has devoured the rot
of a tired soul
and emptied the
crowded spaces
of flesh with air

*new breath
for an old woman
joined to passing
and to timelessness.*

PENUMBRA

Cosmic Pump

The power
of the full moon
does not diminish
because its light
slowly wanes.

The heart does not break
when the blood
it embraces
one moment
is released to the body
in the next.

The sea does not
fall into despair
as its waters
disappear into vapor

The tree is not troubled
to lose it leaves in autumn
when it knows
the season of its glory
is near

It is the nature
of nature
to accept and release
inhale, exhale
receive, give
appear, disappear

In and out of the
cosmic pump
of our inevitable
liberation

The Old Cantos

The old cantos
are strumming
in the wind

No more yesterdays
for tomorrow

the twist quite wistful
in imagined air

and yet so real
to the naked eye

Do not harbor
your small loud
scars

Do not go under
the weight
that carries you

only listen to
the instant

it is mourning

for all that comes
to go
and all that comes
from that.

Coyote Calls

There was a sound yesterday
a million coyote calls
rattling the night

The floundering setbacks
the mismatched hours
stacked against each other

A song lost to
nowhere
utterances
of ash and water
resting
in the cool intestines
of shadow
spring's
illumination
turned to tears

A presence
lost to time
waits for me
in another room

I will be done

A list of wavering betrayals
hang in the closet

Overstuffed hopes
an impossibility of flowers
a child's hand

One more slice
attempted homicide
a certain suicide
of dreams

Someone open the door

Lady Of Lost Causes

Oh goddess
of this strange world

We are sheep shorn
thin and trembling
and lost in the
thorny sands of
Persia.

The map
crumpled kindling
for the fires
of our darkest
nights.

A last dance
on a dithering moment
of scorn.

Weep for us
lady of lost causes
as we resist
the weapons
of our own
destructions

and embrace
the hope
that pins itself
to our enigmatic
shadows.

Just This Once

just this once
the rain slides onto my window like memory
just this once
the wounded healer gives up her wounds to heal
just this once
the star studded amazement of wisdom and truth resonate inside me
just this once
words surround me like ceremonies like sage smoke
just this once
the black obsidian sucks out demons from my breast
just this once
the crystal egg opens to cellular regeneration
just this once
an angel sideswipes my assumptions
just this once
I feel the atoms jumping on my skin
just this once
I see my face behind a curtain of eternity
just this once
the wind pounds a familiar language on my door
just this once
I understand it

Ceremony Coyolxauqui

Moon goddess
woman
black
obscured
divine

Occultress
of night
mistress
of light
unleashed
into
blue
plate night
Offering
of sugar
flame
and of
thin smoke
rising

Enter
the gateway
of flowing hair
portal of leaving

Enter and fill
basket of fruit
glass of water
lake of light

Enter
the circle
Queen
of night
and of souls broken

Enter
create
spiral of stardust

Provide me
your power
my ancient
song!

Ceremonia Coyolxauqui

Diosa de Luna
mujer
negro
oculto
divino

Amante
de planetas
y dueña
de luz soltado
dentro plato
noche azul

Ofrenda de
azúcar, fuego
y de
humo ligero

Entra
la salida
de cabello
suelto
portal de salir

Entra y llena
cesta de fruta

vaso de agua
lago de luz

Entra
el círculo
Reina de rayos
y de almas quebradas

Entra
Creadora de sueños
espiral
de
estrellas

Da me
tu fuerza
mi antiguo
¡canción!

CPSIA information can be obtained
at www.ICGtesting.com
Printed in the USA
FSHW01n2259230818
51618FS